The Joy Ride

IRIS HOWDEN

Published in association with The Basic Skills Agency

Hodder & Stoughton

A MEMBER OF THE HODDER HEADLINE GROUP

A CIP record is available from the British Library

ISBN 0340 688106

First published 1995
New edition 1996
Impression number   10 9 8 7 6 5 4 3 2 1
Year   1999 1998 1997 1996

Typeset by Rowland Phototypesetting Limited, Bury St. Edmunds, Suffolk.
Printed in Great Britain for Hodder & Stoughton Educational,
a division of Hodder Headline Plc, 338, Euston Road, London NW1 3BH
by Redwood Books Ltd, Trowbridge, Wiltshire.

Baz held onto his seat as Andy
swung the car into the fast lane.
The needle reached 90, then 95
– then hit the 100 mark.
'Come on, you beauty!' Andy shouted.

It had been a laugh at first.
Finding the Jag outside the pub.
The door unlocked.
Keys still in the ignition.
'Just asking for it,' Andy said.
'Picture that guy's face
when he comes out!'
He revved up the engine.

'Isn't it risky, taking it in
broad daylight?' Baz asked.
'Everything's a risk,' Andy told him.
'Besides, we're only going to borrow it.
Have a ride, then dump it. That bloke
was drinking. He won't be in a hurry
to report it missing.'

Andy drove out of town,
heading for the open road.
Baz began to relax.
It felt good, to be zipping along,
the windows open, the radio playing.

He ran his fingers over the smooth wood
of the dashboard.
Andy was a great driver, you had to admit that.
He changed gear smoothly.
The engine purred like a cat.

It was on the motorway that Baz
started to feel afraid. A strange smile came
over Andy's face as the car went faster.
He began to weave in and out of the traffic.
He cut in on lorries, taking chances.
Once he overtook a van on the inside,
and the driver had to swerve to avoid them.

Now Andy was in the fast lane
and he put his foot down hard.
'Slow down,' Baz wanted to shout.
'Before you kill us both.'
But the words wouldn't come.
His throat was dry.
The Jag ate up the miles.
Every signpost showed them
to be further away from home.

Then suddenly it was over.
They were slowing down to 50 mph.
Andy braked again and moved onto a slip road.
He drove into the car park of a motorway cafe.

'What's up?' Baz asked.
He was puzzled, but glad they had stopped.
'Didn't you see that police car?' Andy said.
'At the last junction? There'll be another
waiting up ahead. That's how they work.'
'How do you know?'
'I've been done before on this road,'
Andy told him. 'I can't risk getting
caught again. I'll be sent down.'

Baz said nothing. He thought maybe
his mum was right about Andy.
She had always said he was trouble.
'I ought to be getting home,' he said.
'Not yet,' Andy said. 'Let's have a coffee.
Got any money?'
Baz shook his head and Andy frowned.
'Trust you. You're useless!'
He walked to the back of the car.
Baz followed him.
'What are you going to do?'
'Look in the boot. You never know
what you'll find in a Jag.'

He opened the boot and peered inside.
Then he slammed it shut.
His face went pale.
'What is it?' Baz asked.
He had never seen Andy lose his cool before.
Andy opened the boot again, slowly,
an inch at a time.
Baz peered in. He got a whiff from inside.
It smelled like a butcher's shop on a hot day.
'Wow!' he said softly.

In the boot, curled up
like a baby fast asleep,
was the body of a middle-aged man.
He was fat and bald and very dead.
He wore a navy blue suit and had
matching socks on his feet.
'I wonder where his shoes are?' Baz said.

'Never mind his shoes!' Andy shouted.
'Let's get out of here quick.'
He slammed the boot shut and
pushed Baz back into the car.

'Hang on!' Baz said. 'What about the cops?
If we get caught with a dead body
in a stolen car we're in big trouble.
Think about it.'
But Andy was already easing the car
out into the stream of traffic.
'We'll go back on the B roads,' he said.
'Dump the car somewhere quiet.'
Now he was driving as slowly
as someone taking a driving test.
He gripped the wheel so hard
his knuckles turned white.

Baz was really afraid.
He was dying to ask Andy
what they were going to do, but he kept quiet.
Andy had a terrible temper.
You never knew what he'd do.
He might even crash the car.

At last Andy stopped at a rubbish tip
a couple of miles from home.
It was a quiet spot.
Baz wanted to make a run for it
but Andy stopped him.
'There's a little job to be done first,' he said.
'We'd better work fast, before anyone sees us.
Get a move on!' he shouted at Baz.
'Don't just stand there.'
He took off his tee shirt and began
to polish the bodywork of the car.
'Help me get rid of the finger prints,' he said.

Baz begged him to leave the boot shut.
'No way,' Andy said. 'My prints might be inside.
You don't have to look.'
But Baz had to be sure the body was real.
His hands were shaking as he held up the lid
of the boot.
He had never seen a dead person before.
The man's face looked grey.
Blood had run from his mouth and dried
in a brown stain on his chin.
He looked horrible.

Andy looked inside the man's jacket pocket.
There was no wallet. Nothing to say who he was.
'Leave it,' Baz pleaded. 'Let's go,
before anyone sees us.'
'Don't panic,' Andy said. 'There's no-one around.
I want to see if he's got anything worth having.'
'You shouldn't touch anything,' Baz said.
He was near to tears.
'Who says?' Andy scoffed.
'Just because you're yellow!'

He pointed to a gold signet ring
on the man's finger.
'This is a bit of alright. Look,
it's even got my initial on it.
A for Andy.'
He tugged at it. 'It's very tight,'
he said. 'It won't come off. Pity.'
'Don't!' Baz begged. 'Stop it!
What if you were found with it?'
'I suppose you're right,' Andy said.
'Come on, we'd better run for it.'

When Baz got home his mum was sitting
in her dressing gown watching *News at Ten*.
'Where the hell have you been?' she shouted.
'I've been worried sick.'
'Just out,' Baz said, 'mucking about.'
He was too tired to argue.
He went straight to bed, but he didn't sleep well.
In his dreams he saw the dead man's face again.
He woke up in a cold sweat.

In the morning it came back to him –
all that had happened.
He crept downstairs to listen to the radio.
There was nothing on the local news
about a missing Jag – or a dead body.
He watched every TV news. He read
the evening paper from cover to cover.
There was nothing at all about it.

Every night from then on he had the same dream.
It was a horrible nightmare.
In it he was locked inside the boot
with the dead body. He would wake up,
feeling as if he could not breathe.
One night when he woke, his mum was standing
next to his bed. He sat up and began to scream.
She stroked his hair the way
she used to when he was a little kid.
'Ssh, Baz,' she said. 'You were having a bad dream.
Go back to sleep.'

After a few nights like this his mum said,
'I'm worried about you, Baz.
You look terrible. What's wrong?
You can tell me. Are you in trouble?'
Baz hated telling lies to his mum.
They had been close since his dad left home.
So he told her everything.
To his horror she dragged him
to the nearest police station.

They brought Andy in.
The police took statements from them both.
They were kept apart all day.
At last the sergeant brought them together.
'Because of claims made by this young man,'
he said, looking at Baz,
'my men have wasted hours on a wild goose chase.
I don't know what you hope to gain
by telling such fairy tales.
We don't take kindly to people wasting our time.'

'This lad here,' he pointed to Andy,
'denies taking any car.
No Jag was reported missing.
We also made a search
of the rubbish tip you told us about.
We found nothing – except rubbish.
You've been telling a pack of lies.
There was no stolen car, was there?
And no dead body.'

He turned to Baz's mum.
'Take your son home, madam,
and keep an eye on him.
He seems to live in a fantasy world.'
'Thanks a lot,' Andy hissed as they left
the police station.
'I told you to keep it shut – Mummy's boy.'

Baz stayed away from Andy for some
weeks after that.
He felt bad about going to the police.
Nobody liked a grass. He couldn't blame
Andy for being angry with him.

He was surprised to get a phone call
from Andy one evening.
'Something's happened,' Andy said.
He sounded odd. Not his usual bouncy self.
'What? Is it about the Jag?' Baz asked.
'Have they found it?'
'Not exactly. I've got something to show you.
I can't tell you on the phone,' Andy said.
'Can you come over?'
'What now? OK.'

Baz put the phone down.
His mum had told him to stay away from Andy,
but this was important. He sounded upset.
Baz ran round to the flats where Andy lived.
'Come up to my bedroom,' Andy said.
'We can talk there.' He put a tape on.
'So no-one will hear us,' he said.
He looked quite ill.

Baz sat down on the bed.
'What's the matter,' he said. 'What's up?'
Andy reached under his pillow.
He took out an envelope. A plain brown envelope,
with his name and address typed on the front.
He opened it. Something shiny rolled
into his hand. It was a ring.
A man's gold signet ring.

'This came in the post,' Andy told him.
Baz stared at it.
He thought at first that Andy
was having him on. That he'd bought a ring,
just like the one they'd seen on the dead
man's finger, to scare him.

Then he saw the look on Andy's face.
This was no joke. Baz picked up the ring
He turned it round and saw the initial on it.
The capital A. He knew it was the same one.
Baz felt his skin begin to creep.
He hardly dared to look at his friend.
'That's not all,' Andy said.
'There was a message with it.'

Baz heard the fear in Andy's voice
as he passed over a little white card.
Like the envelope, it was typed.
The letters stood out clear and black.
The message was short and to the point.

'YOU'RE NEXT' it said.